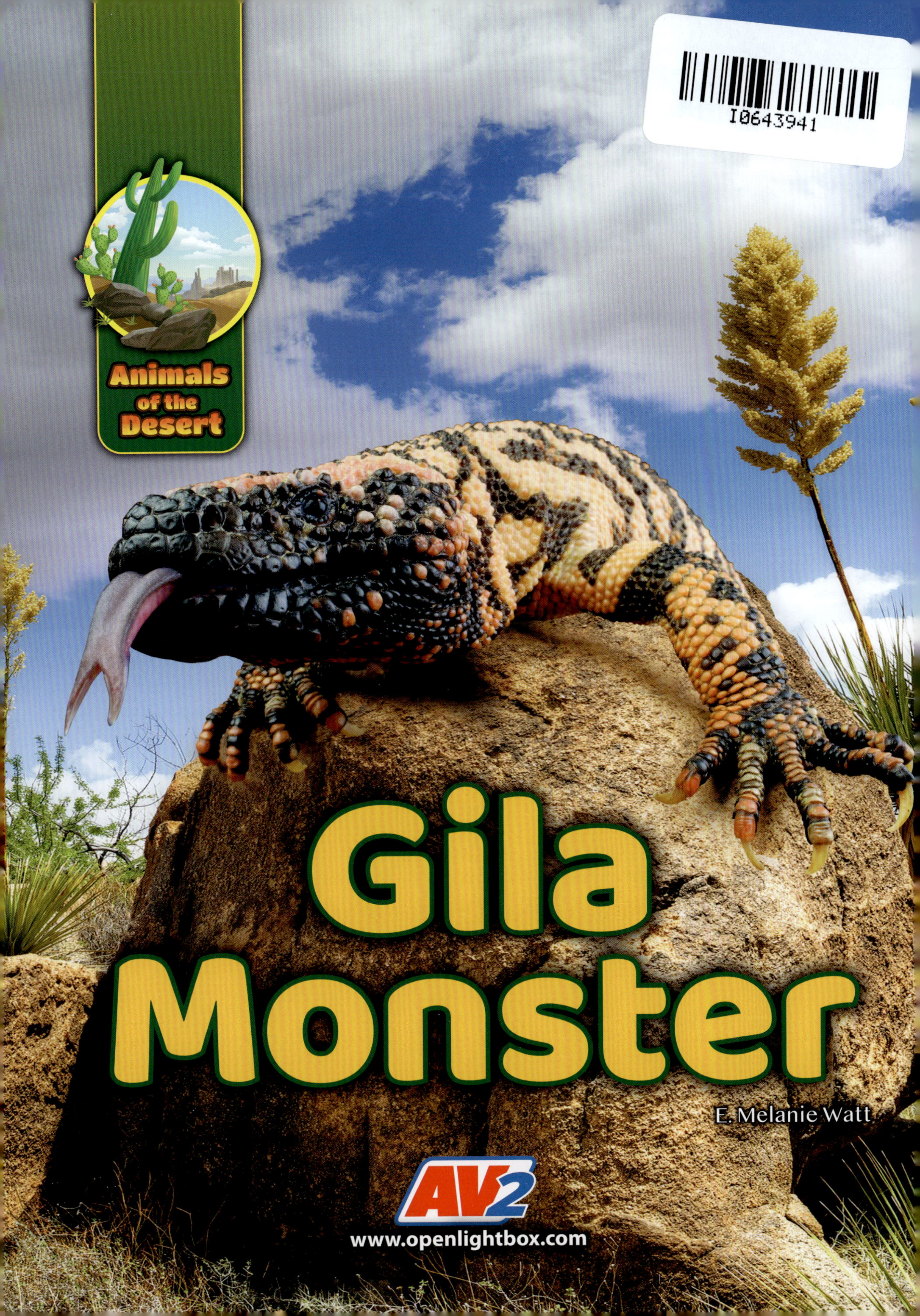

Animals of the Desert

Gila Monster

E. Melanie Watt

AV2

www.openlightbox.com

AV2

Step 1
Go to **www.openlightbox.com**

Step 2
Enter this unique code
SOVJHIW6R

Step 3
Explore your interactive eBook!

AV2 is optimized for use on any device

Your interactive eBook comes with...

Contents
Browse a live contents page to easily navigate through resources

Audio
Listen to sections of the book read aloud

Videos
Watch informative video clips

Weblinks
Gain additional information for research

Slideshows
View images and captions

Try This!
Complete activities and hands-on experiments

Key Words
Study vocabulary, and complete a matching word activity

Quizzes
Test your knowledge

Share
Share titles within your Learning Management System (LMS) or Library Circulation System

Citation
Create bibliographical references following APA, CMOS, and MLA styles

This title is part of our AV2 digital subscription

1-Year Grades K–5 Subscription
ISBN 978-1-7911-3320-7

Access hundreds of AV2 titles with our digital subscription.
Sign up for a FREE trial at **www.openlightbox.com/trial**

The digital components of this book are guaranteed to stay active for at least five years from the date of publication.

Gila Monster

CONTENTS

Meet the Gila Monster

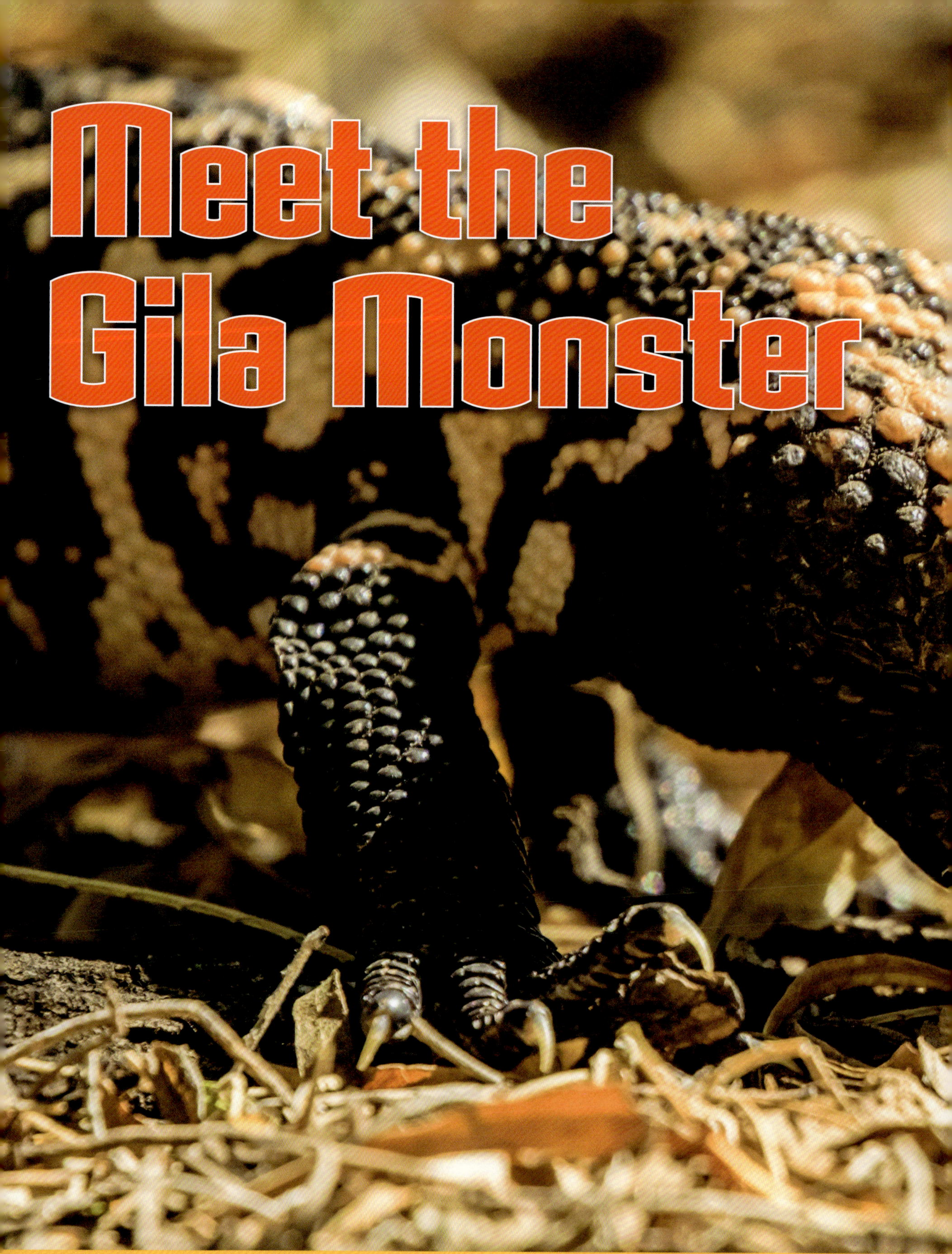

The Gila monster is the largest lizard in the United States. It is one of the few lizards in the world that has **venom** in its bite. Gila monsters have poor eyesight. However, their sense of smell is very good.

Gila monsters are rarely a threat to humans. They tend to move slowly and spend most of their time underground. A Gila monster only bites larger animals when it feels threatened.

A Desert Lizard

Gila monsters can be found in the southwestern United States and in northwestern Mexico. They live in forests, **shrublands**, and deserts. These **reptiles** grow up to 22 inches (56 centimeters) in length.

A Gila monster has strong claws, sharp teeth, and a thick, banded tail. Its body is covered in bead-like scales. Like other lizards, it sheds the outer layer of its skin as it grows.

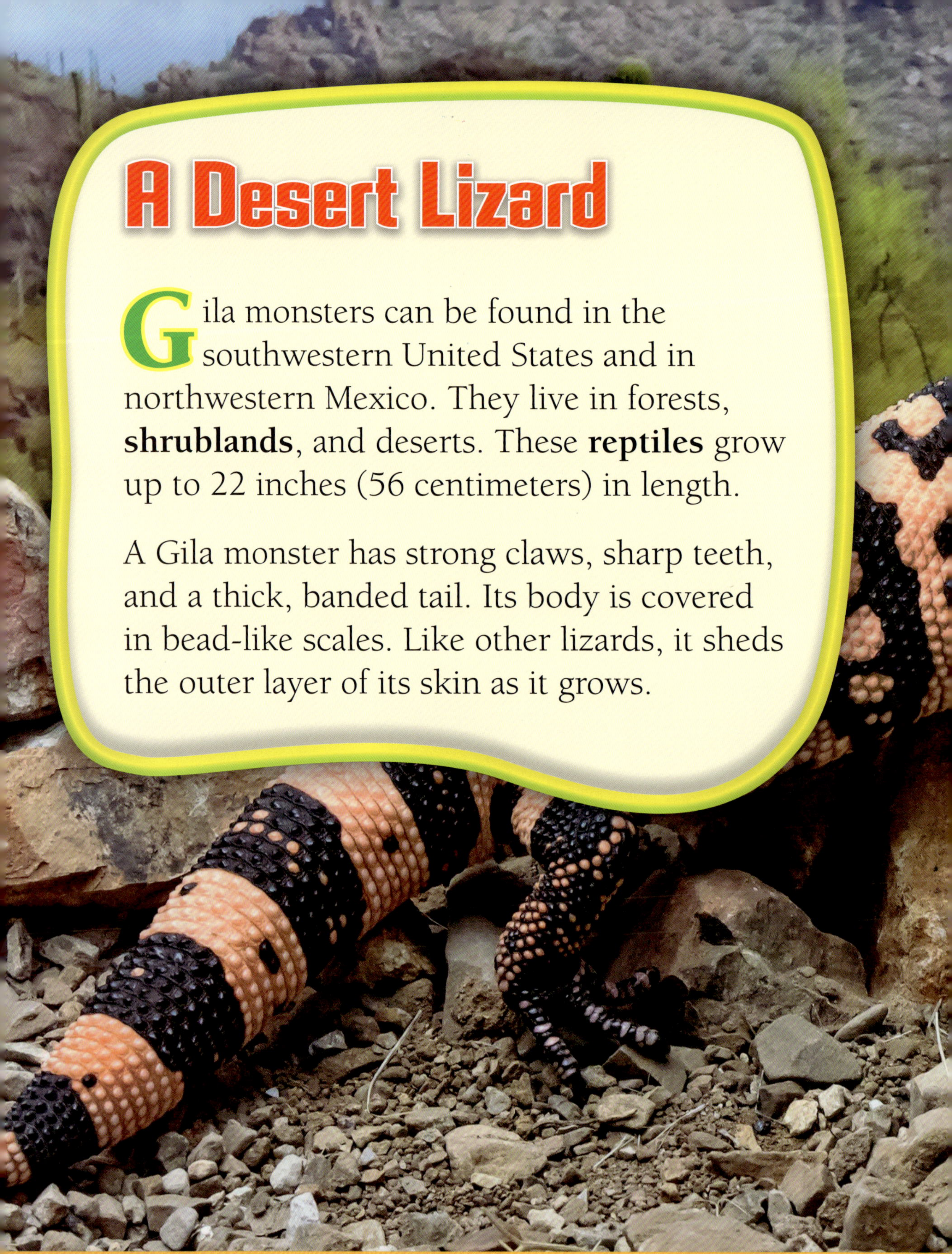

Desert Lizard Lengths
Desert Night Lizard
2.75 inches (7 cm)
Coachella Valley Fringe-toed Lizard
9 inches (23 cm)
Common Chuckwalla
20 inches (51 cm)
Gila Monster
22 inches (56 cm)

Solitary Reptiles

Gila monsters spend most of their time alone. When their mating season begins in late April, they gather together. During this time, males may compete for a mate by wrestling with each other. Matches can last for hours and are a test of **endurance**. The larger and stronger male will usually win. He does this by getting on top of his opponent and pinning him down.

Gila monsters are mostly seen living by themselves. Small groups sometimes gather when resting in sheltered spots.

Desert Lizard Life Spans

Growing Up

A female Gila monster lays her eggs in summer. She digs a hole in an underground burrow to use as a nest. After laying between two and thirteen eggs in it, she covers it up and leaves. Gila monsters do not provide care for their young after that.

Hatchlings come out of their nests in spring of the following year. They are already able to use their venom. This helps them protect themselves.

GILA MONSTER FACT

In winter, a Gila monster will stay in its burrow for **5 months** to avoid the cold weather.

Gila Monster

A Closer Look

Gila monsters have **adapted** to their **habitats**. They have unique features that help them survive in their environment.

Tail

A Gila monster's thick tail is used to store fat. This helps the lizard survive for long periods of time without eating, especially during the winter months.

Scales

Gila monster scales are thick and heavy to help protect the lizard from injury. They come in patterns of black and bright pink, orange, or yellow. The colors may warn **predators** away.

Tongue

A Gila monster flicks out its forked tongue to detect smells in the air. This helps it find its **prey**.

Teeth

Gila monsters have many thin teeth with sharp tips. They use their teeth to break open eggs and to hold onto the animals that they bite.

Claws

A Gila monster's claws are strong and thick. Gila monsters use them to dig for food, such as reptile eggs, and to dig their burrows.

A Powerful Bite

Gila monsters are hunted by predators, such as badgers and hawks. The lizard scares them away by opening its mouth wide and hissing. If the Gila monster still feels threatened, it can quickly bite its attacker and hold on for more than ten seconds. Venom flows from **grooves** in its large lower teeth. It chews this venom into its victim. The bite can kill small animals.

When a Gila monster hisses, it reveals its purple gums as an extra warning.

Life Underground

Gila monsters spend most of their time underground. They live in burrows or rocky shelters, only coming out to hunt for food or warm up in the sun. Gila monsters may dig their own burrows or use burrows made by other desert animals.

In cold winter months, when food is hard to find, Gila monsters stay in their burrows. They live off the fat stored in their tails. In spring, they go outside to hunt again.

GILA MONSTER FACT

Gila monsters spend **90 percent** of their time underground. This makes it difficult for scientists to study them.

Finding Food

Gila monsters are carnivores. This means they only eat meat. While they do not hunt very often, they can eat a large amount of food at a time. The Gila monster relies on its sense of taste and smell to hunt.

Gila monsters often feed on eggs. They climb trees and shrubs or dig underground to find bird and reptile nests. They also prey on small animals, such as insects, frogs, and baby birds. Gila monsters attack other reptiles as well.

Adult Gila monsters can eat prey that is one third their own body weight.

Gila Monster

Gila Monsters in Danger

Some Gila monster populations are decreasing as human development destroys their homes. Another threat these reptiles face is the pet trade. People collect Gila monsters to sell or keep as pets, removing them from their natural habitats. Many areas now have laws in place to protect Gila monsters.

Gila monsters need water to survive. It can sometimes be difficult for them to find enough water in their desert habitats.

Gila Monster Conservation Status
EX
Extinct
EW
Extinct in the Wild
CR
Critically Endangered
EN
Endangered
VU
Vulnerable
NT
Near Threatened
LC
Least Concern
Gila Monster

Gila Monster Quiz

1 Do Gila monsters have good eyesight?

2 How long is a Gila monster?

3 How many eggs does a female Gila monster lay in a nest?

4 What colors can Gila monsters be?

5 How does a Gila monster find food?

6 How does a male Gila monster win a wrestling match?

7 How much can an adult Gila monster eat at one time?

8 What helps a Gila monster protect itself from predators?

ANSWERS 1. No, they have poor eyesight 2. Up to 22 inches (56 cm) long 3. Between 2 and 13 eggs 4. Their scales come in patterns of black and bright pink, orange, or yellow 5. It flicks out its forked tongue to detect smells in the air 6. By getting on top of his opponent and pinning him down 7. One third of its body weight 8. The venom in its bite

Key Words

adapted: changed to suit the environment

endurance: able to continue an activity for a long time without getting tired

grooves: small channels

habitats: places where animals live, grow, and raise their young

hatchlings: young animals that have just hatched from an egg

predators: animals that hunt other animals for food

prey: animals that are hunted by other animals for food

reptiles: animals that breathe air, have scales and a backbone, and have a body temperature that changes to match the surroundings

shrublands: dry areas where only bushes and small trees can grow

venom: a poison made by some animals

Index

Published by Lightbox Learning Inc.
276 5th Avenue, Suite 704 #917
New York, NY 10001
Website: www.openlightbox.com

Library of Congress Control Number: 2023944124

ISBN 978-1-7911-5849-1 (hardcover)
ISBN 978-1-7911-5850-7 (softcover)
ISBN 978-1-7911-5851-4 (multi-user eBook)

082023
101122

Printed in Guangzhou, China
1 2 3 4 5 6 7 8 9 0 27 26 25 24 23

Project Coordinator: Priyanka Das
Art Director: Terry Paulhus

Every reasonable effort has been made to trace ownership and to obtain permission to reprint copyright material. The publisher would be pleased to have any errors or omissions brought to its attention so that they may be corrected in subsequent printings.

The publisher acknowledges Alamy, Dreamstime, Getty Images, Minden Pictures, and Shutterstock as its primary image suppliers for this title.